Killing Myself

By Randy Wilson

\-

Preface 4

Chapter 1 9

Chapter 2 14

Chapter 3 22

Chapter 4 27

Chapter 5 45

Chapter 6 52

Chapter 7 57

Chapter 8 73

Chapter 9 78

Other Books By Randy Wilson 85

Preface

This is the true story of how I killed myself in 2006. The end of a life in most cases is a tragic event and difficult for all who are involved in any way with the deceased. Close friends and family never quiet get over the event when it happens at the hand of the person who has died. Suicide is perhaps the most misunderstood act that one can participate in.

We have entire industries and medial professionals dedicated to the prevention of suicide from counselors on hot lines to dedicated professionals who make it their occupation to help individuals who struggle with thoughts of ending their own lives. Billions of dollars are spent each year world wide in an attempt to provide a variety of support and services to curb the tide of death created by so many different groups of people who keep this industry in business.

The figures on how many people actually take their own lives each year world wide, not to mention the ones who die that we are not sure if it was accidental or not, is continuing to grow at an alarming rate. Those returning from military service often end up not being able to return to a normal life after the military has trained them to be something they were never intended to be and upon returning home they find they can not fit in, hold a job, or eventually find a reason to continue living, and therefore end up taking their own lives.

There are people who are suffering in ways that many of us never see or know about. People being tortured on a daily basis right in front of us that we associate with and know as family and friends and loved ones, and it's not until we learn that they have taken their own lives, that we really begin to think about them and begin to analyze what they were going through and try and understand it and of course by then it is too late because the act of suicide has already happened and that person is no longer with us.

Sometimes it's the young who take their own life; sometimes it's the old. Sometimes it's someone that most of us would have considered and thought of as successful and not really having a problem in the world. Some cases come so unexpectedly that the whole idea of suicide seems to scream at society and demand an answer but like with so many things the answer that do come, come too late to make any difference.

Professionals often feel like they have a good take on the causes and conditions that surround such events and yet with all the professionals and all the counselors and all the shrinks and all the medications available to us, the fact remains that people like myself, choose at some point to stop the pain in the only way that is left to them.

Like any person reaching the end of his rope as the saying goes, there comes a time when there are no more choices and the only thing that matters to the individual is that the pain – the torture they are enduring on a daily basis ends. That is the one thing I can tell you who are interested in the subject of suicide that having killed myself I can tell you that stopping the pain is what it is all about.

People who kill themselves are not selfish as some would like to believe. They are not cowards as some have called them. They are not weak individuals who just refused to pull them self up by their own boot straps as some would have us believe. People who kill themselves have no other choice. They feel that they had tried all the other options to stop the pain and when all options available to them all fail them, they finally take matters into their own hands and put an end to their lives.

That is what happened in 2006. I put an end to my life. Now you may be reading this and saying to yourself, "Clearly he is talking about "Attempted Suicide" since he is writing a book about it, he didn't really die - but I can assure you that is not what I am talking about. I did put an end to my life in 2006. Oh yes, I had attempted suicide on more than one occasion prior to that but when all those failed attempts did exactly that, failed to put an end to me, I like those before me took matters into my own hands and put an end to my own existence.

This book is about the life of one Randall Scott Crossette who I knew personally. He was born the same year that I was born, 1950. Randall who was also called Randy though out his life took his own life in 2006 and I was there when it happened and this is the true story of his demise; for I was a witness to the event and I know the intimate details of how he suffered for many years as we had known each other since childhood.

This book is only going to talk about things that I know myself to be true in connection with the death and destruction of Randall Scott Crossette by his own hand. It is hoped that in sharing what I know about this tragic event that others may find a way to avoid the same fate.

Loosing a close friend to suicide is something you never really get over; at least for me that seems to be true. I sincerely hope by me opening up and sharing Randall Scott Crossette's story with you that you will be able to either avoid his fate yourself or perhaps you can help someone else who is suffering with something similar.

Chapter 1

Randall Scott Crossette was born in Lansing Michigan to his mother Irene Sutherland Arthur Crossett who was married to one George Duane Crossett. Randy as he was called was the second of five children who would be born to this couple here after referred to as - Duane & Irene.

The year date Randy arrived in the world was January 12, 1950. From a young age there was a clear preference for the first born child of Duane & Irene Crossett. He always got the best clothes and it was his older brother David who always seemed to be the child that Duane and Irene were most proud of. I guess there is always something special about your first born child that the following children are never able to really compete with but in the case of the Duane & Irene Crossett family – it was more than that.

I personal knew of stories that happened when Randy was a child that were surely the beginning of the life of torture that he would have to endure. There was the story of the time Irene just barely caught David in time in the second story of the house as he was trying to shove Randy out the 2nd story window with a small handkerchief tied to his back as David had decided if it worked for the little Army men they were dropping out the window, it would also work for Randy and had it not been for Irene happening in on the boys at that moment perhaps Randy would have never had to live the sad life that he eventually did live, due to the fact that Irene stopped the activity.

When Randy was even younger still just a bottle fed baby living in a play pen for the most part, Irene found it curious how Randy was always hungry when she had just given him a full bottle of milk and yet he would be found time and time again crying of hungry as if he had a tape worm or something taking all the nutrition out of him. It wasn't until she witnessed from a distance, hidden from view, her first born child, David, taking the bottle from Randy and drinking Randy's entire bottle and then placing the empty bottle back in the play pen that she began to understand why for so long Randy had been crying seemingly hungry after she had fed him.

David grew up a healthy child where as Randy grew up with vision problems and later other problems that affect him so severely that he had to be taken out of P. E. Classes by the time he was in 7th Grade because his knees were so week no doubt from lack of Calcium he never received as a child in his milk which he never got as a child.

By the time he was 7 years old he was having trouble with his eyes which would affect him for the rest of his life. He wore glasses in an attempt to correct a lazy eye but Duane & Irene were not rich and so after Randy broke several pairs of Glasses they eventually just stop buying glasses for him. Luckily for Randy by then his lazy eye had been corrected but his ability to be in the bright sun affected him from that age on. His eyes would water when he would try to read or concentrate on anything for and period of time and thus his school work suffered and he was not considered a good student.

But like most children, Randy didn't really understand all that had happened to him in his young short life. He was just a kid, like other kids as far as he knew. There other stories I was familiar with that took place when Randy was less than 10 years old. Perhaps the most well known story was the time that his older brother David opened the door and pushed Randy out of the moving car. Of course no one actually saw David do it and since he was the favored first born child no one ever really held him accountable for it, but again it was Irene who noticed that the boys in the back seat of the car had become quiet and so she turned to check on her two sons only to discover that there was only David sitting in the back seat. As she frantically looked for Randy she discovered looking through the back window of the old 1950s car that there was Randy, running behind the car trying to catch up with the car; Blood streaming down his face from where a rock had embedded itself into his forehead when it took the fall from the vehicle.

Of course no one ever bothered to ask David what had really happened and so even though Randy tried to tell them, no one really listened to the details of that tragic event. Everyone one seemed content to have Randy back and was glad that more damage had not been done. Of course the damage to Randy was not just his physical injuries which would be only the first time that Randy would have the pleasure of falling on his head during his lifetime, but the real damage was damage that no one could see physically. Only Randy knew what had happened to him and no one believed him and all just assumed that he had opened the door himself.

Of course no one ever questions why David never reported the incident to Duane & Irene before Irene went looking for the reason the car had become quiet. David seemed perfectly contend at least a few moments, to enjoy being the only child that he always wanted to be.

Chapter 2

Randy lived in Michigan until he was five years old when his father and mother made the big move to Southern California. His father took a job as a linotype operator at a local newspaper in Arlington, just outside Riverside California where Randy would spend the next five years of his life.

During these years the many natural talents that Randy had which his older brother David was completely void of, would become apparent to all.

First of all at the age of about 8 years old Randy began playing the piano. Irene had a nice mahogany spinet piano in the living room of their modest track home. She played from time to time but for the most part it was Randy who put it to good use. Randy recorded how it all began so I will insert that story here so you can hear it in his own words the way he recorded it:

It all started when Randy was about 8 years old and he went down the street to play with his friend Ricky Sleem in the big house on the corner. Ricky was an only child and he was Rich in Randy's eyes. He had a big yard, and a playhouse in the back yard and lots and lots of toys and one day when

Randy went to play at Ricky's house something new was there. Ricky's parents had bought an old upright piano and had put it out in the garage so they didn't have to listen to Ricky play. When Randy got there that day here was Ricky Sleem sitting in the garage playing the boogie woogie on the piano.

Randy was impressed with all the excitement of seeing the other kids gathered around and all watching Ricky Sleem play piano. Ricky Sleem was .... Well he was fat. Most of the kids didn't really like Ricky all that much but he did have the biggest yard in the neighborhood and he had lots of toys and things like the big play house that none of the rest of the kids had, so even though Ricky Sleem was fat and wore big thick glasses and was a Catholic the kids would go to his house to play anyhow because after all... he was the Rich kid and all the kids enjoyed all the things that Ricky always had.

Well this day, the day the piano had been placed in the garage and the day that all the kids learned that Ricky could play the piano; well this day was pretty special. Randy remembered one thing in particular and that was that Ricky for the first time was surrounded by all the girls who wanted to watch him play the piano. The girls didn't usually go to Ricky's house but today was different. There were lots of girls and they all were acting like Ricky Sleem was Ricky Nelson or something! Randy would never admit it, but he was jealous when he saw all the attention that Ricky Sleem was getting from the girls. Randy was a handsome boy and all the girls usually paid him a lot of attention but not today! Today was Ricky Sleem's day to shine. The more Randy watched the more Randy got jealous.

As Randy stood there watching Ricky Sleem play the boogie woogie, he noticed something for the first time in his life. He watched what Ricky Sleem was doing with his hands on the piano and Randy noticed that there were really only about 12 notes on the piano really and that they just kept repeating themselves over and over with some going lower in sound and some going higher, but the keys were all the same and there were only 12 of them. Randy had a piano at his home too but he had never paid much attention to it before that day. He slowly moved up behind Ricky and watched very carefully what Ricky was doing. All the kids kept asking Ricky to play it again, play it again and so Randy just stood there and observed. The kids were talking and saying how nice it sounded and how smart Ricky Sleem was to be able to play piano and read music. None of the kids including Randy could play piano or read music. Ricky had really set himself up as something special this day.

Well finally the jealousy got to Randy with Ricky getting all the attention and Randy opened his mouth and said something like, "Well I don't think it's that big of a deal, anyone can do that if they want to!" And all the girls and other boys there argued with Randy and said things like, "Ok well if you are so smart let's see you do it like Ricky". Well of course he couldn't and so he got embarrassed and as the attention turned back to Ricky Sleem and the many requests to play it again started, Randy quietly slipped out of the Garage and walked home only a few houses away and Randy sat down at the piano that was in his house. The piano in Randy's house was a lot nicer than the old upright that was in the Garage at Ricky Sleem's house.

Randy remembered what he saw Ricky Sleem do on the piano and he put his fingers on the piano and started pressing the keys just like he had seen Ricky do it and ya know what? Randy started to make his piano sound just like Ricky Sleem's piano. Randy thought to himself, this is easy. In just a few minutes having never touched the piano before, Randy was quickly sounding as good as Ricky sounded. Randy didn't know that there were rules about playing piano. He didn't know anything about timing or keys or flats or sharps or scales, all he knew was that if you press certain keys in a certain order just like he had seen Ricky do, that the piano sounded pretty good. Then all of a sudden while he was playing this newly learned boogie woogie song, Randy hit one of the Black keys by accident right next to the white key he was suppose to hit. At first it sounded like a mistake, and then Randy thought to himself, "Hey that sounded pretty good" and so he added that note to what he had been doing.

Randy didn't know you weren't suppose to play just any notes you wanted to but you were supposed to follow what the music said to play. Ricky had a sheet of musical notes he was following when he was playing. But Randy didn't understand the little black things on the paper he was just watching Ricky's hands, so when Randy began hitting new notes some of which he liked and others he thought didn't sound right, he would just alter the boogie woogie as he went along to what ever he though sounded good.

Randy was having fun playing the piano and he was getting excited. He thought to himself, "I'll show that Ricky Sleem! I will practice this until I'm really good and tomorrow I'll surprise them all and then the girls will pay attention to me again!" And that's just what he did. He practiced and practiced and changed and changed that boogie woogie until it sounded twice as good as what the kids had heard up at the corner in the garage.

The next morning Randy put his plan into action. All the kids had gathered at the garage again and again Ricky was getting all the attention from the girls and after a few minutes Randy opened his mouth again and said, "That's no big deal, anyone can do that!" The kids all shouted Randy down and finally said, "Ok Smarty pants, if anyone can do it, let's see you do it!"

Well that is just what Randy wanted. And so he said, "Ok I'll show you!" and he rudely pushed at Ricky who was sitting on the piano stool and said, "Well move and let me sit down". Ricky was used to being told what to do. He sheepishly got up and gave the stool to Randy.

Randy was nervous, well nervous isn't the right word, Randy was scared to death. He wondered if he could remember what he did the day before when he was practicing at home. He wondered if the keys would work the same. Ricky's piano sounded different than the nice piano that Randy's mom had in their home. Randy didn't understand what tuning was all about but he knew that Ricky's piano didn't sound the same as the nice piano Randy had at his house. Well the final stalling moments were over and it was do or die and so Randy put his hands up on the piano and started to play; slowly at first and at first he played it just exactly like Ricky had been playing it. And within seconds Randy's world changed! The kids were all amazed because none of them could play piano, and they knew that Randy didn't know how to play piano yesterday and yet here Randy was playing piano today just like Ricky Sleem!

The excitement grew even more when Randy got comfortable and began adding a few of his new notes into the mix and the girls eyes began to flash and say things like, "Wow Randy, how can you do that? That sounds so good" etc. The more they were impressed and the more they expressed it the happier it made Randy. He had accomplished his goal and had begun a new life as a "piano player" and never again would Randy worry about getting attention from the girls.

From that day forward when Randy sat down at the piano, all the little girls would come running and want to watch and listen to him play. As Randy grew older he only got better. He had the gift people would say. When people would ask him how he does it, Randy would just smile and say something like, "Oh I just push the ones that sound good and leave the other ones alone!"

Randy – David and Debbie 1957

Even though Randy clearly had more talent than his older brother and he was clearly smarter and have more common sense, still it was always David who was the "Older first born Son" that seemed to get all the credit.

When Randy began showing his talent on the Piano David complained and decided he wanted to take Guitar lessons. Duane & Irene were not paying to piano lesson for Randy but for David – if he wanted to learn to play guitar then they would pay for lessons and go out and buy him a steel Guitar.

Well even though it was David who got the lessons it was soon Randy who was not only playing the piano but now also playing the steel guitar and playing circles around his older brother who soon lost interest and could not compete with the abundance of natural musical talent that Randy clearly had.

Then one day something happened that would take any spot light that was left on Randy and shine it all brightly on his older brother who would be come the Hero complete with write up in the newspaper. It happened like this.

Duane and Irene had some close friends named Pat and Paul Robertson who were richer than the Crossett's and they have a big fancy custom home, not a track home, up on this hill and they had a big swimming pool in their back yard. Their home even had different levels inside the home where you could step up or down from one room to another.

One day when David was about 12 years old he was at the Robertson's house when it all happened. Pat the mother looked out her kitchen window to see one of her daughters, Tammy floating face down in the swimming pool motionless. She being a typical mother reacted with a scream which David heard and came running and it was David who pulled the lifeless body from the water and began mouth to mouth as they awaited the ambulance that Pat had called for. To make a long story short, David was credited with saving the child's life and since his father worked for the newspaper there was a nice big write up in the newspaper complete with pictures declaring David the first born child the Hero of the century.

After that event there was little Randy could do to compete. No matter how talented Randy was he would always play second fiddle to his older brother who always got things first, was always old enough to do the things that only he could do because of his advanced age. It didn't matter that when

Duane purchase a go cart for the children to enjoy that David was the only one allowed to drive it even though when David did drive it and flipped it over and caught it on fire and didn't have a clue what to do, it was Randy who saved the day and ran to the rescue of his older Brother who was in a panic and standing there like an idiot blowing on the fire to try and put out the flames. Randy with his common sense grabbed a few hands full of dirt from the parking lot where they had been playing and quickly put the fire out not only saving the go cart from destruction but perhaps saving David's life as the Gas Tank could have exploded which was prevented because of the quick thinking of Randy. But did anyone put Randy's picture in the paper and declare him a hero....of course not.

So that's how life was pretty much for the second born child in the Crossett family. Clearly more talented and smarter but because of his physical size in comparison to David and his position in birth order Randy would always feel second fiddle which was the beginning of depression most likely; A hopeless situation where you can never catch up to your older brother.

It was Randy who would get the hand me downs while it was always David who got the new clothes. And of course now that Debbie had come along the third Crossett to be born, and with her being a female, she not only could claim to be the ONLY girl in the family but she too never got a hand me down in her life. Debbie and David always got new clothes while Randy lived the life of the unnoticed and "unremarkable" child who lived on the scraps from the table for the most part. Did it matter that he was already playing piano at age 10 with no lessons and steel guitar also? Did anyone care that he was already writing poetry before the age of 10?

No! Randy was just the boy between the only girl of the family and the first born child that everyone was always so proud of. The seeds for poor self image and depression and the feelings of never really belonging were sown in the very early years of Randy's life I think.

Chapter 4

Randy In A Band Playing Guitar
1965

As Randy grew older his talents only increase and you would think that from looking at his life he had the world by the tail. He was making good money playing in Bands from the time he was 15 on both Guitar and Organ. In 1968 the band he was in at the time won the Battle of the Bands for the entire Ventura County that year and they were granted exclusive privilege to use any of the musical equipment from the biggest local music store in the area for all their performances and they were given permission to use the store warehouse for their weekly band rehearsals.

Randy got his first car – an Alfa Romeo when he turned 16 purchasing it with his own money saved from his music work. He then left home at 17 years old and attended his last year of high school living on his own in a mobile home park in a trailer he had purchased and was making payments on. At 17 years old he had two renters in his trailer and was working after school at places like McDonald's and the local Hospital and a local drycleaner in Provo Utah.

He graduated from Provo High School in 1968 after totally supporting himself the entire time beginning at age 17.

Randy returned to the Ventura County area and rented a home in Ventura California and continued to support himself by working at a Retail do it yourself Paint store known as Standard Brands in Oxnard California.

At 19 years old having been brain washed his entire life by his family and the Mormon church Randy volunteered to serve a 2 year mission for his church which he again sacrificed all he owned from his pianos to his car to help support the cost of his two year missionary service.

He was sent to Independence Missouri to the Central States Mission, the largest land mass mission in the country at the time made up of all or part of the states of Missouri, Kansas, Iowa, Nebraska, and Wisconsin.

Central States Mission Office Staff
1970
Elder Holiday - Elder Heslop - Elder Crossette - Elder Wagner

During his mission he formed a band in Platteville Wisconsin and played to a crowd of more than 5,000 students at the University of Wisconsin in Platteville. He shared the stage with the popular band of the day known as "The Association" who had come to play a concert at the University and Randy and his band did the 30 minute fill in during the concert where one of Randy's original songs, the first song he had ever written both music and Lyrics for was featured complete with a slide show during the production of the number. You might say it was the first Music Video ever done in the United States as Randy saw all his music in his head and knew how it should look and be presented years before Music Videos were ever produced.

To all who looked from the outside, Randy was living a pretty normal life. Oh he was a creative guy for sure and had a tendency to live on the edge and bend the rules to the point of breaking for sure, but he was for the most part thought of as a very talented handsome young man with a lot of life and spirit about him.

No one knew the emptiness that haunted Randy nor suspected it until he learned to start writing what he was feeling in his fingers on the piano on paper in the form of Lyrics. Only then did the problems that were inside him begin to show to anyone who was exposed to his writing. Randy explained his writing of music like this:

Understanding The Music

I started writing poems at a young age. At the age of 19 I wrote a poem and discovered when I sat down at the piano I could "Play" the poem. Without thought of key, or anything I just sat down and played it. Once I discovered that I began writing Poetry/Lyrics for most all my poetry/music/lyrics which I discovered I could write. I don't really think of it as "Writing" so much as "Translating" the poetry to the musical patterns and rhythms.

I see things in general in life not as they are but as they can be. Poetry is no different. I see a poem and know it's not really complete until its "Translated" into a Musical format. Same as I see a pretty setting and envision a beautiful house or something built on that spot.

Like most I guess most of what I envision never comes into reality but stays in the form of Dreams and Imagination as with many of my poems, they are not set to music yet and others are and are considered by most as not Poems anymore but songs now.

It's all just the same to me. Poems are just songs that have not yet been translated and melodies that don't have words are just musical patterns that need to be translated back the other way and find the words that match the melody until it finally all comes together and is complete.

To me it's no different than building a house. A Bedroom is not a house, a kitchen is not a house and a bathroom is not a house but put them all together and you have a house and put people living in the house and you have a home.

Creating is something that makes me happy to do. I have created houses and I have created homes and I have created poems and I have created songs. As long as I'm creating something I feel my life is worthwhile!

It's nice to hear when people read my poems or hear my music or see something else I created and they feel better for having come in contact with my creations. That's how they make me feel too. Better than before they existed which is why I guess I will continue the work of creation in one form or another until my dying day.

As one of my poems says:

Some men reach for stars

And some just stare

Others stand by and just don't care

Still some others fight to the end

While the rest just pretend!

(Tears I Could Not Find
Written by Randall Crossette
1982 Leona, Kansas)

Now that said this page is going to be dedicated to one song in particular that you will not understand and hopefully after reading this you will appreciate the song more.

This page is going to be all about the song entitled, Family Song 2nd Edition.

Now let's start with the title. Why 2nd edition, well because there was a first edition which was lost. I have had my children tell me many times that they liked the first edition better but at this point in time and life none of us can really remember what the first edition sounded like so it's a moot point now which one was better. I can tell you this, I have lost as much poetry and music as I have posted on this site and that bothers me to think about so I try not to think about it much.

So this was a second attempt to create this musical number and if the first one was half as good as this one is then I'm really frustrated that it's lost but then again let's not think about that. Let's instead talk about this one so you can understand it.

Ok, it's also called Family song because it is written to represent my family and as always there is something to be learned between the lines that don't become apparent until the end of the song.

Ok "How does it represent your family?" you ask! Well to start with each of the parts played are representative of someone in the family. Their place in the family in order of birth, their personality, their talents and what they bring to the table etc are all represented here in the music. It breaks down like this:

Division of Parts on Family song

Left Hand Father

Right Hand Mother

Spirit - First String Part

Rain - Flute

Ryan - Clarinet

Simon - French Horn

Matt - Piano notes back and forth

Nicholas - Second String part

Ammon - High String part (Third string part)

Erik - Trumpet

So this is the idea of the song. As the song starts you hear only ME and my wife. I am represented by the Left hand and what it plays and my wife is represented by the right hand and what it plays. If you listen to it you can see that like all beginning a girl and a boy get married and everything seems to be great and everything makes sense and they work together to make a life which is what the left and right hands represent; Two young people working together to make a life together.

Now you will notice if you are paying attention that the song is like Row Row Row your boat. By that I mean it goes so many bars and then it starts over again and each time it starts over something is added to the mix.

The first time it starts over you can hear quite clearly a beautiful string part and intertwines the music that is already in motion. That single string part that is quiet and sweet is there to represent what most people call the spirit of God or the Holy Ghost or what ever you want to call the light of Christ that is within us that leads us and has influence in our lives teaching us naturally what is right and what is wrong what is good and what is not good.

It's important that you remember this part as the song progresses.

The next time it starts up a Child is added. The first born child in my case was Rain Marie a Daughter and she is represented with her own melody as is each part that is added. Just like in life when you are in a family. Each individual has their own personality and brings something different to the table and each much "fit in" and "work with" the others in the family.

This is what is being represented by the music as it starts with just two people who want to make a life together. The natural guidance of the spirit of God is represented and then as a family grows the children are added; each and individual that is unique.

In Rain's case because she is a girl and girl's voices are generally higher in pitch than boy's voices I choose to represent her with a flute. Listen as she is added to the family making her own way working with and around what the two parents are already doing and you can still hear the direction of the spirit in the back ground. And by the way just incase you are wondering, I don't change the volume levels of any of the parts once they are added. What you hear is exactly how much louder a family becomes, just like in real life as more and more instruments or children are added to the family each competing for space and originality and each competing to be listened to and to be heard and appreciated.

So then comes the next child when the song starts again, which is my oldest son Ryan Seth who is represented by the addition of a Clarinet. Notice how he enters the family, not trying to take over but trying to fit in and blend with his sister Rain yet his lower voice is clearly his own and he goes his own way and he fits right in.

Next time around Simon is added. Now Simon is a totally different son that is Ryan and I choose the French Horn part to represent Simon and notice now how as he enters the mix in the song he is much more demanding and like all the others he makes his own melody that is completely different than mom and dad or the older sister or the older brother and with the addition of Simon the family or the song really starts to come together doesn't it. That's what a third child does to a family. And that third child must be a little more in your face just to make his mark and be heard and appreciated and the French Horn part does that and adds once again to the family mix.

Next comes Matthew my third son. Now I don't want to say that Matthew was a hard child to live with but let's put it like this. Does anyone remember Mork and Mindy the TV show where Robin Williams plays the part of an alien from another planet that comes to earth to live with Mindy.

The point is living with an Alien can be trying and it was trying to live with Matthew until we finally got use to him. Of course once we realized that Matt was really from another planet and that's why he saw life differently than the rest of us we all began to really love and appreciate him, but at first it was hard. In a nut shell Matt was irritating as hell most of the time; it really was just like living with an Alien. Matt just didn't see the world and process information in the same way as the rest of us and that is what makes Matt the man he is to this day.

So because this was written back in the olden days when Matt was still kind of irritating to be around and live with Matt is represented by the piano part which is just two notes that rock back and forth like some nut case banging his head on the wall demanding to be heard and appreciated. Of course he fits in and he is unique to say the least but his part is irritating also like he was back then and that's the story of why his part sounds like it does. That's the Piano notes back and forth back and forth like the ticking of a time bomb or something.

Well after Matthew is added to the mix we really have a bunch of individuals working together but it's still a little rough. When it starts again Nicholas is added.

Now Nicholas is my Jesus Child or at least that's how I thought of him pretty much back then, not sure I still agree with that but lets stay in the right time frame here for the song. Nic's personality was such that unlike Matthew who it took a more refined pallet to appreciate Nicholas was just a peace maker and always smoothed everything out. Nicholas was just a nice kid and everyone instantly like Nicholas every since he was very young. He was just Nic and that was always good enough for him and when he is added to the family the String part which he brings into the family really makes the song start to come together.

Like Nic's personality the string part he is represented by smoothed out the whole composition and that's kind of what having 5 kids is like. By the time you get to 5 kids you know you really do have a family and things out of necessity just begin to work better. Everyone has a part to do and everyone gets their share of time and attention and everyone sees and feels the "We are a family" feeling and that's what Nic's part brings to the song.

Now being the 6th child born the 5 son is not an easy position to be in. That's where Ammon landed in the mix and he is represented also as a String part but his string part is like him...a little "High strung". Ammon is a born "Artist type" personality and he is clearly not like anyone else in the family yet he is a member of that family but what he brings to it is much more delicate and special and so the higher string added to what Nic was already doing, really makes the family complete doesn't it.

But it's not complete yet, there is still another one to come. So the next time the song starts over again here comes poor EZ as I call him. Erik is my last born Child and my 6th son and like any kid could tell you when you are born last and you are number 7 of 7 that have all come before you and got quite a lead on you that can be a very hard position to be in.

So EZ is represented by this Trumpet. Now the trumpet is an instrument that is Hard to ignore if you know what I mean. I mean you don't play a trumpet softly it just doesn't work that way! So I chose the trumpet to show how EZ had to bring up the rear position in the family and how he had to literally scream to be heard and listened to. After all who listens to the baby right? Well that's what EZ had to contend with. He was the baby and he too wanted a place and wanted to be heard and like a baby who CRYS to be heard and to get attention, EZ's trumpet part is very demanding and even though it is he is still almost drowned out in several places by the size of the rest of the family all doing their own things; Each playing his own part, on his unique instrument, in his own way yet working together to make a "Family" work.

Now I will point out to you that on the last verse you can not - no matter how hard you try - still hear the spirit of the lord which you could hear so clearly in the beginning.

That is the secret hidden message of the song. That the challenge in life as you raise a family is to let each add to and get their fair share of attention and appreciation yet try not to drowned out the spirit of the Lord which is still there trying to communicate with you telling you what is right and which way to go but as with life, when you get all the stuff hitting the fan it's hard to keep tuned into that sweet spirit that is playing softly all the time.

So next time you wake up in the morning and the tire is flat on the car and you are running late already and this is the last day you needed to have a problem because of that special meeting you are suppose to be and when you do get the spare tire on and you look at the gas gage only to see you can't make it to work without having to stop and delay even more making you even more late for your special day....well....just remember this song.

That's life. As you add more and more to your family and to your own plate with work and hobbies and other obligations of adulthood the important things sometime just get drowned out in all the noise of everything else.

Mothers I think can relate to this song a lot as they get more and more children and they walk into a room with 7 kids playing and running and screaming jumping here and jumping there. It's hard to remember that each is just playing his part in the big symphony of life that is taking place.

To really understand this you need to go to this link now and listen to the musical composition that I just talked about.

Chapter 5

The young Randall Scott Crossette Family was considered by everyone to be about as close to the perfect family as one could get. They were active in their church and they children were all healthy and nice looking and well liked. Randy spent most of his life doing one of two kinds of work. Either Construction work of one type or another or when that got slow he worked in a variety of local music stores selling digital pianos and keyboards.

He started out right after getting married in 1971 by going to work for his father in law; one Ray Hawkins who live in St. Joseph Missouri. He taught Randy the fundamentals of the Drywall Business and Randy took to the trade like a fish to water. It was only a matter of a few short months that Randy was an independent Drywall contractor himself working on an equal footing with the man who had given him his basis training.

During his 20's and 30's and well into his 40's Randy worked hard to support his large family sacrificing his own dreams of wanting to be able to play music for a living out of necessity of supporting such a large family. His church discouraged him from being in the Music business by pointing out to him that he was expected to "Avoid the appearance of evil" when he came to church wearing the suit coat he had preformed in the night before in a smoky bar and the smell of cigarettes was still lingering on his clothing. Randy had no idea he was being raised in a fanatic cult. Such things as drinking or smoking were considered big terrible sins in the world that Randy grew up in and you were taught to obey and never question the leadership of the LDS Church.

These types of experiences only added to make Randy a more confused individual as he struggle to be a good person, do his job as a father and husband and keep the world around him happy and content when in reality his life and the inconsistencies that were part of it were taking a toll on him both emotionally and mentally.

Still he was considered by all to be a very talented man, with more than an average skill set in a wide variety of areas. During his working years, Randy worked as a licensed Beautician, a licensed insurance agent along with many other jobs that provided him with a vast array of experiences from working as an electrician to working as a full blown Remolding Contractor doing everything from painting to ceramic tile instillation and all things in between. When it came to building by the time Randy was in his Mid 40's he had already owned and done major remodel jobs on several homes and by the time he was 48 and his children for the most part were grown and had left home, Randy was working to build his own dream retirement home on 20 acres in the hills of Arkansas with his two remaining sons still living at home, Ammon and Erik.

It was about that time that a life time of living began to overwhelm Randy. He found himself waking up on Christmas day 1999 a year after moving to this land to discover that his neighbor who had previously given permission for Randy to access this 20 acres -where the home was being constructed - was now revoking that permission and was building a 5 stranded barb wire fence across the access that had been built at considerable expense by Randy.

The change came about due to a feud between Randy's two neighbors who Randy unfortunately lived between. It had nothing to do with Randy except that he became a causality of the war loosing the only working access to his land in the middle of winter.

Randy had been smart enough when he purchased the property to required of the owner a deeded access that would guarantee that he could not be land locked out of his property but had previously as stated gone to this other neighbor and prior to buying was assured that he could access it the easy way across the other neighbors land which is why a lot of expense was spent building the access at the other end of the 20 acres.

But it was a full mile distance this other deeded access and it was not well define, just an old trail that was used for hunting. It would take thousands of dollars and major road construction with Bull Dozers and Road Graders and dump trucks full of road base and gravel to literally build a new road into the 20 acres that Randy and his family called home.

To say that this Christmas day surprise put Randy between the rock and the hard place would be an understatement. He had already just spent the last 2 years doing the impossible. Moving his family from a comfortable rented home in Orem Utah to a raw piece of land which he managed to buy with no money and moved his family on to it with no power or water lines available on the property; Totally raw undeveloped land.

Randy's boys accepted the adventure quite well as boys will do and during the first year live in small Camping tents and had only self made outhouses for toilets.

The extent of the miracle that had been sacrificed for by all concerned is almost beyond words or belief that he was able to make it all happen at all, but that is what Randy was known for doing; the impossible. What other knew could not be done Randy looked at only as something that could be done with enough work and effort and sacrifice and he had proven that he could create something out of nothing many times previously in his life time. This time was to be no different but this time it was supposed to be his last big project; the property he would develop and the home he would build from nothing with no money this time was to be the home he would spend the rest of his life living in. The home Randy expected his grandchildren would come to visit him in but like so many of Randy's dreams in life, this one was to end differently than expected due to circumstances totally out of his control.

No one could have seen it coming. Oh there were hundreds of songs and poems Randy had written during those same years expressing the emptiness he felt, the terrible sadness that increased with the years and it's easy now to look back and say, "Someone should have got him some help" Hind sight is always 20/20 but Randy was such a miracle worker all his life, that the things he wrote just never seemed all that important to anyone.

They were clearly indications in his writings that things were not right inside of Randy himself but again, he had become such an expert at making the impossible happen and turning 1 dollar in to 100 dollars and he had proven everyone wrong so many time before being able to adapt to any new challenge given him, when Christmas 1999 arrived with is last straw surprise it came as a total surprise to everyone.

What would take place in the next year would be even more unbelievable but having witnessed it myself, I can assure you that this all happened just as I'm telling it to you.

Chapter 6

The ten years prior to the year 2000 appeared to be good
years for those who were spectators from the outside looking
in. Randy was busy with his music production Studio
known as Heart Studios. He was writing and producing and
recording. He was working at one of the largest music
dealerships in Utah. Again Randy was doing what others
only stood by and watched in amazement from a distance
wishing they had as much courage, faith, and determination
and skill to be able to make their dreams come true as they
perceived Randy was constantly doing.

But those years were not a bed of roses. And the fears that
were implanted in Randy from his radial cult church
experience were coming to a head. Randy had been taught
all his life to prepare for disaster; the end of the world; the
return of Jesus Christ the day when all the prophecies would
be fulfilled.

Indeed the very world Randy grew up in supported the idea
that the world was quickly going to the dogs. Randy grew up
in the cold war era of the United States. As a young man
Randy experienced things like the Cuban Missile Crises and
was traumatized by such events as the JFK assassination

and the Vietnam War. He grew up in the 1960 when it was all about drugs sex and rock and roll and indeed there were many in the world, in other religions who were predicting the end of the world as we know it.

It was a common held belief by many of the time that the end of the world would be happening by the year 2000. This lifetime of experience of worrying about Russia pushing the button, the constant threat of possible nuclear world war, the storage of food, even the training as a child how to get under your desk in the air raid drills that were practiced in the public school. These events and the constant religious teachings that the end was near, even at the door all mixed together to make Randy feel that being prepared for the end by being out of debt, in a place where he could raise his own food and have animals like chickens and pigs and cows was the right thing to do.

These pressures drove Randy to do the miracles that others saw him create and moving to Arkansas to a raw piece of land in 1989 was seen by some as extreme but other particularly with in his religious support community admired and respected his effort to prepare for that which was surely to come.

So when 1999 arrived, Christmas Day, after a lifetime of working, worrying, and stressing out over trying to obey the leaders of his church, follow the counsel and teachings of the "prophets" which included having a 2 year supply of food and clothing and water for your entire family, a task that was impossible for Randy to accomplish with his large family and lack of wealth, still it was expected of him and though it had taken almost 30 years of craziness, radical teachings and religious training in a cult to bring him to this point, is it any wonder that when Christmas 1999 arrived with the events of that day that Randy finally snapped.

Unable to make sense of it all from the lies he had been taught as a child to the world coming to an end but never really quite happening, to the dealing with all the fear and inability to do as he was being told to do; not able to accomplish all that was expected of a good righteous man to care for and prepare his family for the hard times Randy has spend a life preparing for and stressing out over. It all came to a head that Christmas day.

It's easy to look back on those years and read the many things that Randy wrote and expressed in his poetry and music and think, I should have know something was wrong; there must have been something I could have done to prevent this tragedy from happening. As Randy's closes and indeed his only true friend, I still carry some guilt for not having been more educated and aware of what I might have been able to do to help him. But alas in the end, I failed him like everyone else and that which was put in motion on Christmas Day 1999 would within a few more years end with the total destruction of Randall Scott Crossette. A great loss that I don't have words to describe at this point in time.

One thing I can tell you is that Randy was a worker. I never knew a man who could work so hard and so long and work circles around everyone else on a job. At times it seemed he was nothing short of super human but as I suppose it is with all super hero's Randy was about to run up again the kryptonite that would change him from a Hero to someone who no longer was with us.

Chapter 7

Randy had only 6 more years to live but he had no real way of knowing that as none of us do for the most part. After Randy was hospitalized for clinical depression it was only a matter of a few months before his wife of 30 years, the mother of his 7 children, the woman he had build his whole reason to exist around would get on a bus and walk away never to return.

Was it the fact the she was embarrassed to have a husband who was now considered mentally ill having been diagnosed while in the hospital as everything from a Borderline personality disorder to major reoccurring depression to a Bi polar personality?

It didn't seem to make any difference to anyone that Randy following his nervous breakdown had gone to counseling and was taking medications as directed and doing all he could to regain a semblance of normality in his life, it seems that nothing he could do would change the events that were put in motion on that fateful Christmas day.

Perhaps it was just the fact that his wife didn't want to live in the remote area in the home Randy had built for his family in the hills of Arkansas that was the reason she boarded the bus that day under the pretence of visiting their only daughter who was due to have a baby soon and living back in Utah a half a world away from Arkansas.

Maybe just the living with Randy the miracle worker for 30 years was just the limit of what the woman could take. I suppose we will never know what was going on in her head when she left that day on the bus but in the end, she never returned, never spoke again to Randy, and didn't even bother to show up for her own divorce hearing which was held almost a year later. Randy was granted divorce on the grounds of abandonment just one more experience he did not need after all he had been through to that point in his life.

He was now 50 years old, alone and on his own. Like always he had little to nothing to begin with as his wife took the home she swore she would never take from him, built with his own two hands and blood and sweat. But when divorce happens, things that you never thought possible happen too and so who could have perceived or predicted that Randy's idyllic family would turn on him and actually shun him as taught to do by the cult he was raised in.

Randy would now be considered an Apostate, and as such, it was right to separate your self from him and have nothing to do with him anymore. The fact that he was your father would mean little to nothing to good Mormon children. They would do as the LDS church directed in this matter and so Randy found himself quickly more alone in the real sense of the word than he had ever been in his life.

Randy had been excommunicate from the LDS church who had caused so many of his problem - basically for being now officially mentally ill. No other explanation was ever offered. This meant that the whole world in which Randy had been raised in and all the people connected with it whether family or friends were gone; All but one. A good friend who remained his friend right up to the end came. I guess I have to admit I was not his only friend; he has another whose name is Reed Guymon who once employed Randy as an Electrician's helper. Randy always credited Reed with everything he knew about electricity.

So at 50 years old, now taking what he felt was needed medication according to the professionals, Randy was totally on his own with no family that wanted to talk to him, only one friend and so in an effort to change his world, Randy ended up going to the Philippines to start a new life and leave all the negative things behind him. His first trip to the

Philippines was in September 11th of 2001 following the finalization of his divorce.

Randy had already spent a year alone on his land in Arkansas, and the isolation was not good. Randy needed a life, a new life, and the only thing he knew for sure it that the last 50 years of his life had been pretty much wasted. At least that is how he saw it. I don't know if I agree with that or not but I would not want to have gone through what I saw my friend experience in life.

Randy had managed to get on Social Security Disability due to his classification now as officially mental ill and unable according to the doctors who saw him to hold a job anymore. So he was granted his Social Security Status beginning at age 51. It would be only a few short years before he would put an end to his life by his own hand but for now it seemed Randy was on top of the world.

Randy quickly found a companion in the Philippines and was married. Falling back into the only life he had ever known. It didn't last long, less than a year, and soon Randy had been cleaned out of everything he had managed to save from his divorce and 50 years of life in the USA. It was a good lesson for him but after all he had been though already, he was now a man alone again with very little to live on.

Randy eventually returned to the USA and continued with taking medications and went to counseling and tried to get his life together but met with little real success. After several years of living with depression and talking with counselors he made the decision to put an end to it all.

Randy being the kind of guy he was, put a lot of thought into how to end his own life. He didn't for example want to traumatize others who would have to find him. So something as simple as a bullet in the head was out of the question. To messy and not fair to who ever had to discover him. He finally after long consideration, decided that the best way would be to die of an overdose of sleeping pills. The pills were being provided to him because he had trouble sleeping and so it would be easy to get enough pills to swallow. That seemed to be a good way to go anyhow he concluded. Just go to sleep and wake up hopefully in a new world where things were not as they were in this world for him.

But knowing how was not enough information to suit him. Like with everything, Randy always thought things through and tried to find the "Right way" to do something. He had been raised in a church and was constantly exposed to doctrines that taught him as the LDS Hymn "Choose the Right" says, "....choose the right, there is a right and wrong to every question"

This black and white thinking was something Randy had internalized many years prior to the end of his life. For Randy there was a right and wrong for every question and it was his job as one of the good guys, which is how he viewed himself, to find the right way. Not just to kill himself but that was something he lived by. It never mattered what Randy wanted so much or anyone else for that matter what was important was always to know and do "What was right."

These types of questions might seem strange to you but to Randy they were just normal. Randy knew that according to what he had been taught killing himself was not right. But if he was going to do that which was not right, he still had to do it the right way, the best way, because he would not want to add on to the condemnation the fact that he did something wrong and then on top of that did it in a way that hurt others or made things worse.

Perhaps when you look at that kind of thinking you will agree with those who said he was mentally ill. But for someone raised in the LDS church even if they throw you out for being of no use to them anymore the indoctrinations that you have received over the last 50 years had a tendency to stay with you. If anyone out there has had to deal with a family member who has been part of a cult and then tried to get them away from that situation, you know what I'm talking about.

So whether Randy was legitimately a mental case of not, this was how he was thinking during that time. He finally decided that the best way to put an end to his life would be to go to another country, where no one knew you, and get rid of all your id so you would not be easily or quickly identified, and just go to some random hotel and take your bottle of pills and go to sleep and let the maid find you in the morning. That wouldn't be so bad he decided.

And thus Randy made arrangements to visit the Dominican Republic for the soul purpose of finding a place to die and end his own life. He only spent 30 days there but that 30 days showed him something he didn't realize until then. The reality was that he had so much fun visiting there, he decided rather than to prove everyone right and kill himself which is what his family expected him to do, he would live to spite them. Live to be a thorn in their sides. Continue with his life and just make a new life for himself; one last miracle you might say.

The problem was that he was still so depressed that he was unable to stop crying most of the time. He had been talking with counselors and writing music and poetry trying to get it out and deal with what he was feeling but it wasn't enough. By the time October – November of 2005 arrived Randy had not only returned to the USA with his failed attempt to end his life as planned but now had despite all the medication and counseling slipped back into a deep depression that he was just not able to pull himself out of even with the help of all the professionals and medication.

He was meeting with several shrinks and counselors and being tested for this and for that. He found himself finally living in a homeless shelter in the winter of 2006. Randy had shared with his counselor that he was sure he would not make it past Christmas that year that he could no longer stand living with the endless hopelessness, loneliness, emptiness and pain which comes with depression and at his lowest point he wrote the following two songs

Step by Step

By Randall Crossette

Step by Step I walked this world of darkness all alone

Step by step I find that I am farther from my home

Step by step each broken dream, the dreams I called my own

They vanish right before my eyes like I'm a sinking stone

Step by step I try

Step by step I cry

The dreams I dream

A waste of time and never to be mine

The Water's deep I can not swim it's useless but I try

The rain it comes and soon a flood of anger from my eyes

I can not see what's wrong with me won't someone lend a hand

I need to know before I go that someone understands

Step by step I try

Step by step I cry

The dreams I dream

A waste of time and never to be mine

I want to say a word or two to those who think they know

The cross I bear its all despair and such a heavy load

You do not know, you are not me - you can not understand

For in my world I'm all alone

A lifetime one man band

One step forward two steps back

One step to step aside

One step to get over it

One step was such a lie

One step to get through it and

One step to step in time

The choice to take the last step now is mine

I only want to see the light to know that it is there

I'm tired of the constant pain and darkness I find here

Like walking from a darken room to light that's what they say

I hope they're right I don't need disappointment not today

One step to get past the pain

One step that I will hide

One step just to cover all the lonely tears I cried

One step just for me I need to put a stitch in time

One final step to step across the line

Forgive me won't you please dear Lord I know you understand

You know that I was never meant to be this kind of man

The ship has sailed the song is sung my symphony is done

All good things end and as you know the time for me has come

One step up to lay it down

One step without a sound

One step just to free my soul

One step to sacred ground

One step closer to the end

One step to get around

Just one more step and I am heaven bound

Repeat the three last choruses

One step forward two steps back

One step to step aside

One step to get over it

One step was such a lie

One step to get through it and

One step to step in time

The choice to take the last step now is mine

One step to get past the pain

One step that I will hide

One step just to cover all the lonely tears I cried

One step just for me I need to put a stitch in time

One final step to step across the line

One step up to lay it down

One step without a sound

One step just to free my soul

One step to sacred ground

One step closer to the end

One step to get around

Just one more step and I am heaven bound

And just before leaving for the Dominican Republic he wrote this one:

http://theworldaccordingtorandy.com/Nothing%20to%20believe%20view.html

Nothing to Believe

By Randy Crossette

2006

When I was just a boy I learned my ABC's

I trusted all they told me

I dreamed of life to be

I trusted with my Heart

I gambled with my soul

Eternity seems such a worthy goal

Have faith in all you do

And never doubt a thing

Faithfully follow along and sing the song we sing

Who could have guessed the day

That life would empty be

That faith in God would make a fool of me

And now you wonder why

An angry hearts inside

A man with Faith set free

With nothing to believe!

Tomorrow is a gift - that none can guarantee

And yesterday is dead and gone and matters not you see

Today is what is real in sunshine or in rain

And what is real is love is all in vain

So turn and look away

Believe I've gone astray

Tell yourself I'm wrong

And go and sing your song

A picture can not lie - Nor can my heart repair

The music says I'm empty and there's nothing left to share

I'm close to being through - I know the end is near

I'm just about all out of empty tears

So judge me if you will

I've had more than my fill

I gave it five more years

And still there were more tears

They say that it's all me Perhaps it meant to be

They say that it is selfish and they know what's best for me

Like Judas long ago - the part is just for me

Like Judas I now go to find my Tree!

It was now close to the end and Randy was desperate to find
a way to end it once and for all. The depression was just too
much and that's a fact that many do not understand about

Depression I think. People who kill themselves don't do it but for one reason and that reason is to stop the pain.

Randy had to find a way to stop the pain, enough was enough and in the fall of 2006 after returning from the Dominican Republic he was struggling with the last days of his life trying to find a way to end the pain and also trying to do the right thing; two irreconcilable facts.

Chapter 8

Randy finally decided that to live and spite his family was his best option but the depression that Randy suffered from would not allow him to live much longer no matter what he wanted. Someone had to stop the pain and thus far none of the medications were working, none of the shrinks or counselors had the answer and so once again Randy found himself totally alone in the world to find a way to solve his problems. No one was going to be able to help with this one. Randall Scott Crossette needed to die; it was the only way the pain would end. There was no other option. The time was now limited as the depression was pulling him down more each day. Living in a homeless shelter in the middle of winter wasn't helping either. Randy got an idea one day.

What if he was to Change his name, and become legally and totally a new person and do away with Randall Scott Crossette and all his problems? Randy had really loved living in the Philippines and felt that if he had to start a whole new life as a new person that is where he would like to do it. There was no longer any reason to keep hoping that his children would change their minds and begin having contact with him again. They were all being good little cult members shunning their wicked apostate father and that was not going to change.

So with again only the small amount of money he was getting from his early Social Security payments and with no legal experience or knowledge of how to actually accomplish this new goal and with limited time, Randy set out to kill himself. To put an end to Randall Scott Crossette and all that was connected to him.

He went to the public library and talked to people and learned what it would take for him to legally change his name to something else. He made a list of each and every thing he had to do in order to put an end to Randall Scott Crossette and to return himself to a place where he could start his new life for real, not as Randall Scott Crossette the mentally ill and disabled person of before but as a new person with no problem, no hangs ups, no cult teachings to direct his life, a new person who could learn for himself what was right and what was wrong.

He started down the list. There were many things on the list that needed to be accomplished. There would be money needed for another plane ticket. There would be money needed for filing papers with the court. He would have to eventually replace everything from his Social Security number to his Drivers license to his passport. He put things in the order they needed to be done and then worked his list one item at a time until the day came.

December 4th 2006 Randy walked into a courtroom and with the slap of a hammer on the judges' desk Randall Scott Crossette ceased to exist. He had the paper in his hand with his new chosen name that was the key to everything else.

He went directly from the court house to the Social Security office located in town and had his name changed on his Social Security number to his new chosen name.

From there he went to the DMV and with the documents necessary in hand he was able to get a new drivers license with his new name and they took his old license and destroyed it.

From there he applied using his newly created ID for a new passport and sent those papers off.

He was living at the time now in an old house where he had got employment remolding the home for another old man. He was being paid in cash and he had talked the man into letting him live in one of the rooms he had finished in the basement so the man didn't have to come to pick him up every morning at the homeless shelter.

Randy returned to his temporary home where he still have work to do and money to earn to be able to complete his plan.

That Christmas came and went and Randall Scott Crossette did not make it past Christmas of 2006 as was predicted. He came to an end on December 4th 2006.

It was strange at first for my friend to have a new name and it was even stranger for him when he realized that he could no longer prove he was his former self. The only thing all his ID from Drivers license to Passport could prove was that he was this new named person on all his ID.

The day it really hit home was the day he got his first Credit card in the Mail. Randall Scott Crossette could not get a credit card if his life depended on it. He was poor and had a large family and had no good credit history. But this newly created person, created with nothing more than a judge saying it was created, it had no credit history. This new person was starting with a clean slate and if my friend needed anything to prove that to him, holding a brand new shinny Visa credit card with a $500 credit limit on it was that proof that he was no longer Randall Scott Crossette.

By the first part of February of 2007 the final stage of the plan was to be put into motion. My friend would return to the Philippines. No longer in need of medications – No longer suffering from depression – no longer carrying the burdens of one Randall Scott Crossette – For Randall Scott Crossette had been killed off both physiologically and legally and now there was only the new man, with his whole life ahead of him and free to make his own rules and his own life now based on what he felt was right not what someone else told him was right.

Chapter 9

As you might have guessed by now, this true story is the true story of my own life. I am now John Randall Wilson. The name picked for the following reason. I wanted still to be called Randy and the two other names John and Wilson are two of the most common names I could think of which was why there were chosen. I no longer wanted to be Randy anyone...I just wanted to be Randy from now on and that is how most people know me to this day.

After all my trips to and from the Philippines since 2001 following my divorce in the USA, I finally came back to the Philippines a new man; a man who was no longer burdened with the problems that Randall Scott Crossette had.

Am I cured you ask? Well I will admit that I was pretty messed up after the first 50 years of my life. I have since studied and learned how to treat clinical depression naturally and I live with a better understand of my own chemical make up. I understand the importance of getting out and going for a walk and getting the sun shine on my face.

I also understand that depression does make you physically tired and sometimes you need more sleep than a normal person and the difference is now when I'm tired I let myself go to sleep and I sleep for as long as I feel I need to before I make myself get out of bed again. I no longer feel guilty if I sleep for 16 hours and then that is followed by 24 hours of being awake and working. I no longer pay any attention to the clock or the calendar. When I'm hungry I eat and I have learned not to just eat for entertainment which has allowed me to get control of my weight and be more healthy than I was 15 years ago.

I live in a country where everyone considers me their best friend and wants to have me over to their house and wants to tell their friends that they know me and have spoken to me. I'm basically treated like a celebrity is treated in the USA and I can't think of a better natural medicine for depression and self image problems than that.

Randall Scott Crossette wrote his last music years ago now. I have no need to write music anymore. There is nothing I'm trying to get out anymore -, I have let it all go. I can still write poetry and I do and have and I have learned to write and publish books on the internet.

I have retained the best parts of Randall Scott Crossette and left everything that was negative behind in the past. I have very little contact with my children. Some of them still have not spoken one word to me in 18 years others I have sporadic FB conversations or a few lines of information passes between us.

Does that bother me, well it use to but not so much anymore. I understand I raised my children in a cult church and they are doing what they have been taught to do and so I don't worry much about that anymore.

It's true I have not met but one of my many grandchildren and never will but I have written many books now and they are published and available for them to read when they reach the age that they want to know more about the Grandfather they never had in person.

I no longer worry about the end of the world, or look at ever event from the Earthquake & Tsunami in Japan to the recent Earthquake and Tsunami that his this country and almost wiped Tacloban off the map killing thousands, as signs of the times that are something I need concern myself with.

Do I still believe in some kind of Religion you might ask? I would answer you this way. I do not believe in any organized religion and I'm of the opinion that the world as a whole would be better off without any of them. So I don't attend a church or foolishly give my money to such con jobs anymore, I now spend my life just trying to be a good person. Instead of just going to church every Sunday and spending hours talking about how a person should live and how they should treat others, I now spend my life trying to put all those words into action on a daily basis.

I personally donate at least half of my personal income to my own charity projects so I'm constantly feeding people, buying medicine for people, paying for school fees, the list just goes on and on and eventually every month I run out of money and start over again the next month.

Unlike the way Randall Scott Crossette lived his life, a life lived in constant Fear of the end of the world and lived in Fear of what "others think of me" particularly the others that I shared space with in the cult...all that is no longer part of my life. I don't concern myself with the "Words of the Prophets" of the LDS church who tell me to store a 2 year supply of food etc. Now when I have resources I spend them as I think they should be spend and that is to help someone who is right in front of me who is hungry or naked or in need of some other kind of help.

Am I a Christian and do I still believe in Christ and the Bible? I would answer that this way. I am sure that the Jesus known to this world as the Christ who was killed some 2000 years ago was real. And I'm still of the opinion that he is probably who he says he was and I try to follow the example that he set in how to treat and deal with other people in life.

As far as me worried about my soul or being saved etc? No I don't worry about that anymore. I wasted enough of my life worrying about things that I had no control over. I now trust that if there is a God and I'm counting on the idea that there is, that he is a Good guy and will treat me right if I have treated others right. Of course that is just what I choose to believe whether it is true or not I won't know for sure until I die and find out what if anything comes next.

Like you I hope there is something that comes next but now that I have lived the life I have lived I can honestly say that I have no fear what so ever of death. I don't wish to live longer nor do I wish to end my life any longer. I'm content to just be thankful for what I have today and for the good I can do together to those around me.

That is enough for me now. If I die tomorrow that's ok with me and if I live for another 20 years I guess I will have to live with that too won't I, since I don't really have much control over that do I?

Oh yes I could go back to the way that Randall Scott Crossette once thought and consider ending my own life, but now that I'm not him, with his problems I don't feel any need to think that way anymore.

I don't particularly like getting old. I'm not sure anyone like getting old but I'm taking it in stride. I presently do not live with any companion and I have enjoyed my time alone and been able to accomplish a lot because I was alone and didn't have someone else I had to worry about. Whether or not I will take another companion during my life that remains to be seen I guess.

The one thing that is nice here in the Philippines is that if you are an American and you have a stable income which I do, you are pretty much still considered a good catch at any age, so just knowing if I really wanted a companion I could at the drop of a hat choose one – that makes my life good too just having that knowledge.

What are my plans from here on out you ask? No big plans just try and keep helping people as I can. Enjoy my life as much as my health allows me to do that. Keep writing books about my life and about the Philippines and try and share with others via this format things I think might be of value and interest to them; So no big earth shaking plan to change the world.

I enjoy hearing from my readers who come from all over the world so if you have enjoyed this book please feel free to write to me and make comments or ask questions.

thephilippinetravelreview@gmail.com

Other Books by Randy Wilson

Living In The Philippines 2014

http://www.amazon.com/dp/1495297314

The Philippines

http://www.amazon.com/dp/B00EEA8VTE

10 Great Reasons To Retire In The Philippines

http://www.amazon.com/dp/B00FBG8Q0E

A Vacation To Remember In The Philippines

http://www.amazon.com/dp/149278883X

Vacation In The Philippines On $10 A Day

http://www.amazon.com/dp/1492346756

Paying for Sex or Marriage & Divorce

http://www.amazon.com/dp/1495428966

For a complete list of Randy Wilson Books

www.amazon.com/author/randywilson

Click on the "Books" Tab

www.ingramcontent.com/pod-product-compliance
Lightning Source LLC
Chambersburg PA
CBHW070259290526
45791CB00003B/1005